WILD CHILDREN

CONTENTS

CHAPTER 1

WILD CHILDREN

At one time or another, nearly everyone has heard about "wild children"—people who grew up without human contact. In some cases, these children were even said to have been raised by wolves or other wild animals.

This painting is based on the Roman myth of Romulus and Remus, who were supposedly cared for by a female wolf.

Folklore and Fiction

One such tale from Roman mythology is that of Romulus and Remus, the twin brothers credited with founding Rome. According to the myth, these royal infants were set adrift in a basket on the Tiber River by their uncle, who felt the boys might one day claim their birthright and depose him.

The twins were washed ashore, where they were found by a female wolf that cared for them along with her pups. The boys were later said to have been taken in by a shepherd and his wife, who raised them until it was time for them to fulfill their destiny.

There are numerous similar stories. Tarzan, a fictional hero portrayed in a series of books and films, was supposedly raised by a female ape in the jungle. A jungle in India is the setting for Rudyard Kipling's *Jungle Book*—another classic story in which a young boy is raised by animals.

▶ *A scene from an animated film version of Rudyard Kipling's* Jungle Book *showing the bond between humans and animals*

▲ *A photo from the film* Greystoke, the Legend of Tarzan, Lord of the Apes, *in which an infant boy is raised by apes*

11

Real "Wild Children"

While these tales aren't true, they seemed more believable after reports of present-day "wild children" began to surface. These include the 1962 account of "Djuma," a young boy discovered running with a wolf pack in Russia's bleak desert region in central Asia. When a group of men spotted the boy and threw a net over him, the wolves rushed to his defense. As a result, the animals were killed, and the child was sent to a **psychiatric** research hospital, where he remained for the next thirty years.

During that time, he described to doctors how before he had learned to run on all fours, he would ride on his wolf mother's back when the pack hunted. However, Djuma had been at the hospital for several years before speaking his first word. It was even longer until he slept comfortably in a bed. Decades after being taken from the wolf pack, he would still eat only raw meat.[1]

There was also the story of the six-year-old boy from Kenya who was repeatedly seen scavenging for food with a wild dog. As a toddler, the child had been abandoned by his mother, a coffee-plantation worker. After being captured, the boy referred to the **canine** as his "mother" and indicated that the animal had looked after him.[2]

In 1984, still another report of a wild child became known. This time, a Chinese news agency revealed that the youth had slept in a pig **sty** and been suckled by pigs. The baby was originally left with the family's pigs because

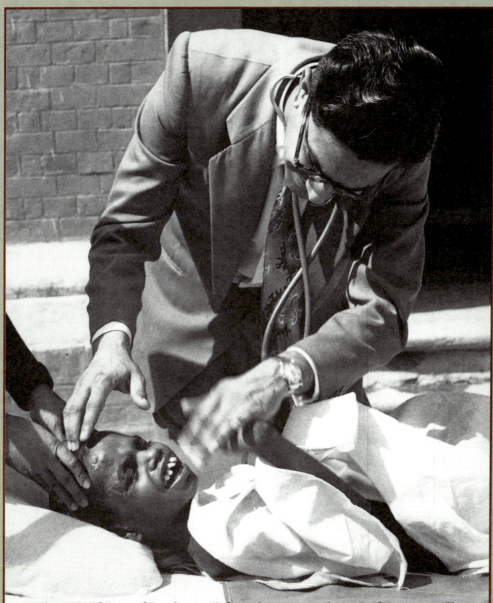

The "Wolf Boy of Lucknow," found in a jungle in India, was still another child said to have been reared by animals. Doctors who examined his body felt he might have once lived in a wolf's den.

the baby's deaf-mute father and **mentally retarded** mother felt unable to care for a young person. Until age five, the child had survived on almost nothing but **sow's** milk.[3]

Although humans have long had pets and raised farm animals, the thought of the reverse—animals caring for humans—seems incredible. It is an area that has never been scientifically studied, since to deliberately place an infant in a wolf den or pig sty just to see what happens would be morally unacceptable.

Yet every so often, something occurs accidentally that provides a glimpse into what could happen. One such incident took place the summer of 1996 at an Illinois zoo, when a three-year-old boy fell over a barrier into a gorilla exhibit. Eyewitnesses reported that a female gorilla picked up the injured boy and cradled him in her arms. While shielding the child from the other gorillas, she brought him near a door where he could be readily rescued by zookeepers.

The animal's unexpected mothering behavior makes us wonder how being "adopted" by another species could affect a human's development and future. This book is about children who were not raised by humans. In some cases, they were thought to have lived with animals. In other cases, they were purposely isolated from the people around them. Their stories provide a fascinating look at a world rarely seen.

CHAPTER 2

FOREST CHILD

*I*t was the late 1700s in France, and for several years, the villagers of Aveyron had gossiped about a strange occurrence in the surrounding woods. A number of people claimed to have glimpsed a wild being darting through the trees. No one was certain whether it was human or beast, but some thought they must have spotted the same naked creature searching for roots and acorns to eat.

This scene from the film The Wild Child *shows what the forest child of Aveyron might have looked like when living alone in the woods.*

Were the stories true, or just the work of overactive imaginations? Many people weren't certain until September 1799, when three sportsmen venturing into the woods seized the creature as it scampered up a tree to escape. To their surprise, the mysterious being turned out to be an eleven- or twelve-year-old boy.

The child was like nothing they had ever seen before. His naked body was covered with scars, and his long hair hung from his head in a tangled mass. The boy's teeth were extremely long, and yellowed as well. There was nothing **civilized** about him. When cornered, he raged, snarled, bit, and spat. Obviously unfamiliar with toilets, the youth urinated and defecated wherever he happened to be standing.

The "wild child," as he was referred to, was left in the care of a widow living nearby. But within a week, he broke loose and ran away. He avoided capture for months, spending the winter roaming the surrounding mountain ranges. Once in a while, someone saw him and reported that, even in the freezing cold, he wore only the now-tattered shirt he had been given for warmth.

Yet when spring came, the wild boy surprised everyone by approaching nearby villages. One day, as he accidentally wandered into an inhabited house, he was captured for the second time. Now he found himself unable to escape, while his future rested with a group of people who could not have been more unlike him. The

In this scene from the film The Wild Child, *the young boy is caught for the second time.*

wild boy's existence raised a number of important questions for doctors and scientists of the day. Could he provide valuable clues about what humans would be like if kept apart from civilization? Could someone adopt human ways after spending his or her entire youth in the wild?

"A Completely Animal Existence"

In September 1800, the wild boy was brought to Paris for scientific observation. A group of scientists there hoped to find out how much the boy could learn, as well as what could be learned from him. The general public was anxious to see the child as well. But the boy's eagerly awaited arrival in France's capital city disappointed many. Throngs of people had flocked to see him, expecting to find a "noble savage."[1] The sight that greeted their eyes, however, led them to believe that the youth was more savage than noble.

The dirt-encrusted wild child rocked and swayed back and forth endlessly as though he were a caged animal. He bit and scratched those who cared for him and was indifferent to everyone else. Communication was nearly impossible. Upon his arrival in Paris, the wild boy had remained completely **mute** except for some occasional **guttural** sounds he uttered in response to nothing in particular.

If the youth disappointed the public, he didn't do much better with the professionals evaluating him. Philippe Pinel, a well-respected French educator and **psychologist**, was

19

Philippe Pinel was the first professional to examine the wild boy following the boy's arrival in Paris in September 1800.

the first to examine the boy. His findings were not very promising. He felt that the child's natural abilities were similar to those "of our domestic animals."[2] He further noted that the child lacked the attention span to focus on any one thing more than momentarily, and was unable to distinguish between a real object and one in a picture. Pinel also found that odors had no apparent effect on the boy. Whether he was smelling an expensive French perfume or sniffing his own **excrement**, the child's facial expression never changed.

Try as he might, Pinel found very little that was "human" about the young forest person. He described the boy as having "a completely animal existence" and claimed that the wild child "differed from a plant only in that he had the ability to move and utter cries."[3] Pinel concluded that the youth was probably severely retarded. He had worked previously with mentally retarded children and felt that the similarities between these young people and the wild child were too obvious to ignore.

Yet not everyone in the scientific community was quite ready to give up on this unusual case. The actual task of educating and "civilizing" the boy fell to the director of France's National Institute of the Deaf and Dumb. The child wasn't **deaf**, but no one knew quite where to put him. The director, in turn, assigned the job to a twenty-six-year-old physician named Jean-Marc Itard, who had been working at a nearby military hospital.

Jean-Marc Itard, the physician who spent five years working with the young forest boy

A drawing of the "Wild Boy of Aveyron," who was later called Victor

Itard's Efforts

Itard relished the opportunity. While there had been scattered reports of wild or **feral** children throughout history, no doctor had ever had the opportunity to study and work with such an individual. If Itard succeeded in easing the wild boy's path into society, he would be the toast of scientific circles throughout the world. Thinking he had found his road to fame, Itard devoted himself wholeheartedly to the project at hand.

Although Itard respected Pinel's opinion, he refused to immediately accept that the boy was mentally retarded. He knew that retardation was an incurable condition limiting the extent to which a child could learn. Itard tended to think of his unruly pupil's limitations instead as a result of the child growing up deprived of much of what makes people human. This was a condition he hoped to remedy by working closely with the boy.

After observing Victor (the name given the wild boy), Itard classified the child's existence as consisting largely of "sleeping, eating, doing nothing, and running about the fields."[4] In working with him, Itard noticed also that he appeared indifferent to heat and cold. At the sight of newly fallen snow he might run from his room half naked to play in it. He could remain outside for hours, romping and rolling in the snow—even eating it with gusto. The same lack of sensation applied to extreme heat. Victor could pick up a burning hot coal or potato from the fire without so much as blinking.

Here, in a scene from the film The Wild Child, *Dr. Itard tries to teach Victor to use a key.*

For five years, Itard spent every day working with Victor, but in the end, he was unsuccessful. His attempts to involve Victor in creative play failed. Once, he gave the boy a set of bowling pins, hoping that the child might enjoy knocking them down and setting them up again. But Victor remained completely uninterested and tossed the playthings into the fire. The boy eventually learned to say one or two words, but he never really understood their meaning. Victor's memory also seemed extremely poor. Itard routinely showed him a number of objects and repeated their names, yet the child could not recall what they were.

In the years spent with Itard, Victor did make some limited progress. He developed a warm relationship with his governess, Madame Guérin, and learned to use gestures to some degree to make his needs known. But Itard realized that Victor had probably progressed as far as he'd ever progress. By then, Itard had begun to accept the likelihood that Victor had been abandoned in the woods as a very young child because he was mentally retarded. No one could explain the large scar on Victor's throat. Itard wondered if someone could have cut the child's throat and left him for dead in the woods. Could it have been that Victor had unexpectedly recovered and miraculously survived on his own?

A Sad End

In any case, Itard called off his experimental work with Victor in 1806, noting that by then, it had become little more than a trying exercise for both the boy and himself. He wrote: "I hoped in vain. All was useless. Thus vanished the brilliant expectations which I had founded."[5]

Victor's life ended as sadly as did his teacher's dream. He left the school for the deaf to be taken in by his governess, Madame Guérin, who lived down the street from the institution. He was never able to find his place in society, and the remainder of his life has been described as "a grey forlorn existence."[6]

CHAPTER 3

MYSTERY CHILD

If the European public was at first fascinated by the unexpected appearance of a wild child among them, they did not have to wait long for it to happen again. In May 1828, a teenage boy wearing tattered peasant clothes was seen staggering through the streets of Nuremberg, Germany. Exhausted, hungry, and thirsty, he could barely walk.

The city of Nuremberg, Germany, as it might have looked when Kaspar Hauser first arrived

Just as the boy was about to collapse, a passerby rushed over to help. It was hard to understand what the tired and confused boy was trying to say. However, since the boy was carrying a letter addressed to a local army regiment captain, the passerby took him to the captain's home.

The captain was away when the boy arrived. The house servants, after looking at him, thought it best that the teen sleep in the barn until the master's return. They soon found that the unusual-looking boy also had unusual eating habits. The cook gave him a piece of meat, but after just a few bites, his face twisted into spasms and he spit out the food in horror. The same thing happened when he tried a mug of beer. He did, however, seem to greatly enjoy a tall glass of water with a piece of bread.

Kaspar Hauser

When the captain came home, he was unable to learn very much about the boy. By then it had become obvious that the child didn't know how to speak. He seemed only able to say something that sounded like—"I want to be a rider as my father is." When questioned as to where he came from or who his parents were, he would gesture to indicate that he didn't know.

The letter to the captain said that as an infant, the child had been taken in by a family that already had ten children. The person who wrote the unsigned letter claimed not to know who the boy's mother was, but added that for financial reasons he could no longer care for the youth. The note ended with the suggestion that the boy be trained as a soldier.

Although the local police carefully scrutinized the letter and questioned the boy, they weren't any more successful in finding out about him. There were only two clues to his possible identity. The letter indicated that the boy was born in 1812, and when given a pencil and paper, the child wrote the name Kaspar Hauser. Unfortunately, that would be the only information anyone had to go on for some time.

This note was found on Kaspar Hauser when he was first spotted staggering through the streets of Nuremberg, Germany.

A drawing of Kaspar Hauser dressed in the fashion of the day

Kaspar Hauser was taken in by the Hiltel family of Nuremberg. While with them, he made some remarkable strides toward fitting into society. Although he was once described by a spectator as a "brutish and inexpressive savage," Kaspar learned to dress fashionably as well as to walk and carry himself properly.

It was Julius, the Hiltel's eleven-year-old son, who first taught Kaspar to talk. The two played together often, and in time, Kaspar acquired a limited use of language. However, his general education and language development was left largely to Professor Daumer, a teacher who devoted most of his time to assisting the boy.

Kaspar's Past

In some ways, speech helped to at least partially unravel the youth's mysterious past. Through a series of conversations with the town's mayor, Herr Binder, Kaspar revealed that his early life had been spent in a large, cage-like cell. For the most part, his was a dark, silent world. He couldn't recall hearing any sounds or being able to tell whether it was day or night. Each morning when he awoke, he would find his daily ration of bread and water. Once in a while, his water tasted strange. On those days, the boy would sleep longer than usual. When he awakened, he would find that he had been washed, his fingernails cut, and his clothing changed. The only playthings he was ever given were two wooden horses decorated with ribbons.

Kaspar Hauser recalled that at times, an older man came to see him in his cell. The older man taught him how to write his name—the only thing Hauser could write when he arrived in Nuremberg. The man also sometimes held him by the waist and raised up his body as if he were trying to teach Kaspar to stand and walk straight. The boy thought the man was not unduly cruel, though he recalled that just days before he was taken from the cage, the man beat him with a stick.

Kaspar Hauser remembered little of his trip to Nuremberg. All he knew was that the journey took several days, and that most of the way, he was bound and carried over a man's shoulder. It was obvious to those now caring for him that for much of his life, Kaspar Hauser had been unlawfully imprisoned. Unfortunately, the youth was unable to let anyone know where this had occurred or who was behind it.

Kaspar's Progress

In numerous ways, Kaspar Hauser thrived in his new environment. Even so, the boy always remained mentally and socially behind other youths his age. His vocabulary was still quite limited, and he had trouble understanding concepts such as size and distance. When walking away from

A portrait of Kaspar Hauser after he had become accustomed to civilization

a tree, he actually believed the tree became smaller instead of just seeming that way because he was farther from it. Other things confused him as well. If he saw a woman whose scarf was dragging along the ground, he would call her "the lady with the tail."[1]

Nevertheless, Kaspar genuinely enjoyed living in a community, and later went to stay with Professor Daumer's family. This way, the pupil and teacher could spend even more time working together. Hauser advanced rapidly in this rich intellectual setting. In describing the boy's educational strides, the professor said, "He was diligent in learning, increased in knowledge and made considerable progress in ciphering and writing."[2]

Mysterious Enemies

Yet these advances may have eventually caused Kaspar Hauser's undoing. As word of his achievements spread, it was widely rumored that he was about to write his biography. Actually, this was just a page or so of disjointed half sentences rather than the real details of his background. But at the time, the general public didn't know this. Anyway, shortly thereafter, someone tried to kill the youth. Professor Daumer's wife was on her way up to Kaspar's room when she saw blood on the cellar door. She opened it and found a bloody trail leading down the stairs. In a corner of the cellar, Kaspar Hauser lay silently in a pool of his own blood.

At first, Mrs. Daumer thought the boy was dead, but Kaspar clung to life. The doctor was called and indicated that there was a good chance that he would pull through. Kaspar Hauser spent the next two to three days delirious. He was unable to identify his assailant but did say that the man wore black and had kept his face covered. Kaspar had no idea why anyone would want him dead. While delirious, he called out, as if speaking to his would-be murderer, "I all men love; do no one anything. Why the man kill? I have done you nothing. . . .You should have first killed me, before I understand what it is to live. . . ."[3]

While recovering, Kaspar Hauser remained with the Daumers. However, those close to the boy were concerned about his safety. They feared that whoever had tried to kill him might return to finish the job. For his own protection, Hauser was sent to live with an English family. He was given another tutor, but he never had an opportunity to use what he learned. Shortly before Christmas 1833, Kaspar was approached by a stranger on the street. The man beckoned to the youth, claiming that he had information about Kaspar's mother's whereabouts. Unfortunately, the promise was a ruthless trick. As the youth came closer, the man stabbed him in the chest and ran off. Hauser died three days later.

Kaspar Hauser's mysterious death posed some serious questions. Why did the youth become a murder target? How could a deprived, uneducated boy like Kaspar be a threat to anyone? It was later revealed that Kaspar Hauser's real-life story might be more complex and intriguing than anyone had imagined.

The explanation most often given for Hauser's assassination was that he had not really been an abandoned child as was indicated in the letter he brought to Nuremberg. Instead, it was believed that Kaspar was the **legitimate** heir to Germany's dukedom of Baden. Supposedly, he had been kidnapped at birth by conspirators who wanted another relative as duke. Those close to the infant were told that the child was dead, but he was actually locked away in a dark cell.

Once the preferred heir was in power, Kaspar's captors released him. Since the boy could utter only a few words and had lived in **isolation**, they felt they were safe. But when it was rumored that Kaspar was about to write his life story, the culprits panicked. If Hauser were somehow able to tell the details of his inhumane imprisonment, their own lives might be in question. The assassination, therefore, became the final phase of their deceitful dealings. With his life abruptly cut short, no one will ever know how much Kaspar Hauser might have accomplished. In more than one way, his story remains a mystery.

CHAPTER 4

THE WOLF CHILDREN

*H*ave all the "wild" children discovered through the years been boys? No—girls who have grown up in the wild or with almost no human contact have been found as well. One such case, involving a Christian *missionary* and his wife, took place in India in the 1920s.

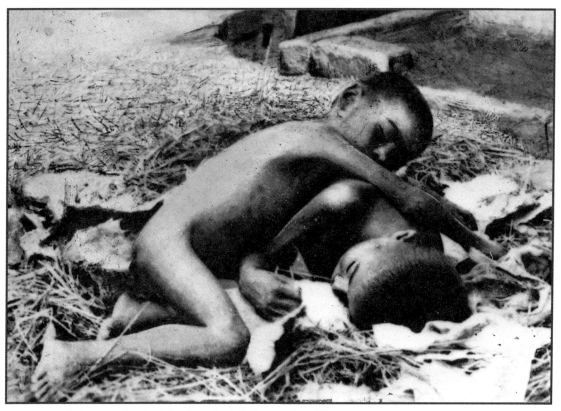

The two feral girls slept huddled together like pups.

Missionary J. A. L. Singh was first alerted to a problem when local villagers told him that a "man-ghost" (a figure with a human body and the head of an evil spirit) had been seen in the jungle. After organizing an expedition to see what the "man-ghost" really was, the missionary came across the source of the villagers' concern. He found two feral girls who had been living with a female wolf and her cubs in a wolf den.

A female wolf cares for her pups at their wolf den. It appears that Amala and Kamala found shelter in a similar setting.

Amala and Kamala were found in a jungle in India like the one shown here.

Amala and Kamala

It was easy to see why the villagers had not immediately known that the children were human. The pair walked on all fours as wolves do, and their bodies were covered with sores and scars. Their **unkempt** hair had become badly matted and covered most of their faces. When discovered, the two children were huddled with the wolf cubs as if they were pups. The missionary and those with him took them from the den and brought them to the orphanage he and his wife ran. They then set about the enormous task of helping the children adjust to human society and a life entirely different from the one they had known.

The Singhs estimated that one of the girls was about eight years old, while the other one was probably only about eighteen months. They named the older child Kamala and the younger one Amala, but the Singhs knew that giving the girls human names was just a first step. They also had to make them look human. The children were bathed and the massive tangles cut from their hair. The Singhs also attended to the girls' immediate health needs. As the Reverend Singh described: "They were covered with a particular kind of sore all over the body. My wife and myself used to wash the sores with carbolic lotion and carbolic soap and bandage them with boric cotton. . . ."[1]

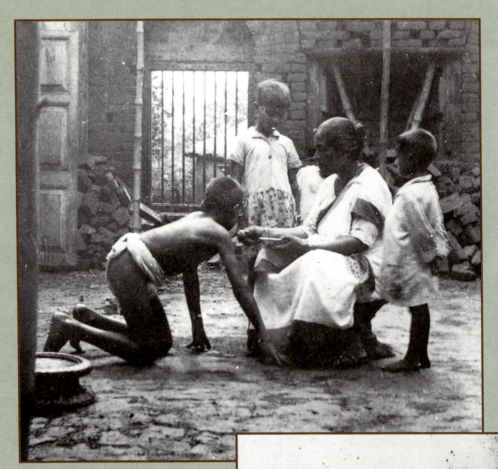

▲ *Finding it difficult to learn the ways of human society, the feral girls walked on all fours.*

The feral girls would eat only from a plate on the ground. ▶

Life with the Singhs

Despite the Singhs' efforts, the girls clung fiercely to their old ways. This made it extremely difficult to care for their medical needs or form any type of meaningful relationship with them. The Singhs tried to expose Kamala and Amala to other children, but the two always remained close to one another, shutting out everyone else. Whenever anyone tried to approach them, they made faces, showed their teeth, or let out harsh, piercing cries.

In observing the girls, the missionary and his wife noticed that Kamala and Amala had acquired a number of distinct animal-like traits. Both children could squat down on the ground, but their joints had grown too inflexible to allow them to walk upright. Instead, Kamala and Amala moved about the orphanage on all fours. It also appeared that the girls had finely tuned senses, as they were able to smell freshly killed meat from a distance and could detect sounds too faint for most humans to hear. In addition, their eating habits were quite similar to an animal's:

> They used to eat or drink like dogs from the plate, lowering their mouths down to the plate. . . . When they were hungry they would come smelling to the place where food was kept and sit there. The least smell of meat anywhere, even a dead animal or bird, would bring them to the spot at once.[2]

Mrs. Singh tried to "tame" the children, as she called it, by showing them affection at every opportunity. At times it seemed as though the pair were beginning to trust her. When the girls were frightened, Mrs. Singh was the only person they would turn to. Mrs. Singh also used praise to encourage them to speak. Here, however she was less successful. After a year, the older child only occasionally answered Mrs. Singh with a grunt. This failed to develop into anything close to human speech until some time later.

Despite the Singhs' hard work, it was obvious that the girls preferred living in the wild to living with other humans. While at the orphanage, they tried to escape several times. The missionary recalled one of their attempts:

> When they wanted to get away, a girl named Rhoda prevented their escape. They gave her such a bite and scratched her. . . . They ran just like squirrels and could not be overtaken. . . . It was really a task to search them out, because they remained noiseless there until they were discovered. [3]

Kamala Alone

Unfortunately, in September 1921, both children became extremely ill. Although the older girl recovered, the smaller child died. The Singhs were saddened by Amala's passing, but the death was hardest on the older girl. She had to be pulled away from her friend's body and for the next few weeks just sat in a corner. Months later, she was still seen sniffing the places where Amala had sat or slept.

In her last years at the orphanage, Kamala took some

▲ *Amala and Kamala were good climbers and had mastered other animal behaviors as well.*

▶ *This photograph shows Kamala standing for the first time. Reverend Singh holds her head to help her stand upright.*

Although Kamala eventually wore dresses, she still often sat alone, facing the wall.

Reverend Singh with his wife, the staff, and the children at the orphanage

important steps towards being like the other children. She wore girls' clothing and developed a vocabulary of about thirty simple words. Yet in many ways, she remained more like a wolf than a human. She never learned to use her hands to handle food, but continued to eat with just her mouth off a plate on the floor. Sometimes she would visit the orphanage's dogs at feeding time. They didn't growl or bark at Kamala but allowed her to eat from the portion given them. She was never caught killing an animal, but if she found a dead bird she would grab it and run off into the bushes. When she reappeared the bird would be gone and there would usually be some telltale feathers around her mouth.

Although the world eventually learned of the "wolf-girls," the Reverend Singh and his wife had originally tried to keep their existence secret. They feared that if the girls' background became public, it would be hard for them to one day find proper husbands. In India in the 1920s, a woman's only hope for a secure future was through marriage.

Obviously, the Singhs had hoped that the girls would arrive at a level of human behavior that neither Amala nor Kamala were able to reach. As it happened, it didn't matter. Kamala, the older child, died at the age of about seventeen after battling a serious illness. At the time of her death, she was still more comfortable with animals than with humans.

CHAPTER 5

THE LOS ANGELES GIRL

If you think that finding a child raised in nearly total isolation could never occur in modern times, you are wrong. One such tragic case came to the public's attention in November 1970 in Los Angeles, California, with the discovery of a thirteen-year-old girl named Genie (not her actual name).

According to police reports, the girl's elderly parents had kept her locked in a room tied to a potty chair for most of her young life. Restrained by a short rope, she sat alone on the floor, never learning to speak or be with other people. A social worker on the case noted that when Genie was found, she was wearing a diaper and uttering **infantile** sounds.

Help Arrives

The child was taken to Children's Hospital in Los Angeles. There, a team of professionals would try to see if an intensely warm, loving, and educational environment could possibly make up for a life of deprivation and despair.

As with other "wild" children, at first Genie did not present a very **optimistic** picture. She spat constantly, and sniffed and clawed at nearly everything around her. It was later learned that while at home, Genie had been severely beaten for making noise. As a result, those working with the girl found that she was usually silent.

Yet despite the unusual way she dealt with the outside world, Genie had a knack for drawing others to her. Said David Rigler, a psychologist at Children's Hospital, "I think everybody who came in contact with her was attracted to her. She had a quality of somehow connecting with people. . . . She had a way of reaching out, without saying anything, but just somehow by the kind of look in her eyes."[1]

Besides helping Genie to start a new life, the hospital staff hoped to learn more about the long-term effects of such severe isolation as hers. Jay Shurley, an expert in social isolation, has singled out **solitary confinement** as the most severe punishment that can be given to a human being. He stressed that it can negatively affect a person within only a few hours or days. Researchers wondered if Genie's brain waves had been altered as a result of her prolonged solitary confinement and if she had suffered any permanent mental damage due to living under those conditions most of her life.

A young girl takes part in brain research just as Genie did.

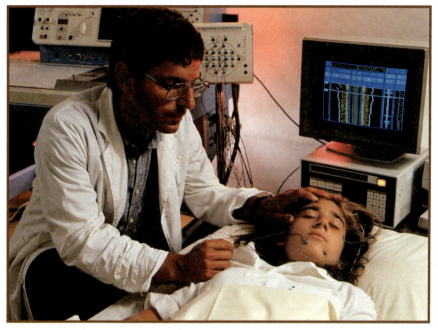

A doctor studies a teenager's brain waves. Genie worked with a number of researchers to further their knowledge in this area.

So that her brain waves could be studied, Genie slept wired to instruments for four nights in a row. As expected, the researchers detected an abnormal brain wave pattern. Genie had an especially high number of dense bunching patterns that looked like spindles on a spinning machine. The pattern was common to brain-damaged or mentally retarded individuals. Yet these test results left the researchers with still another question. Was Genie born mentally retarded, or did she become that way as a result of the extreme isolation she experienced?

Because of Genie's unique background, it was difficult to learn very much about her early childhood. Genie's mother, a fragile, nearly blind woman, claimed that she and her daughter had been controlled by her headstrong, domineering husband. Supposedly, Genie's father had decided that his daughter was "slow" as a baby and insisted that she remain hidden from the world. When Genie's plight was discovered, he committed suicide.

The Genie Project

The health-care professionals working with Genie had ambitious plans for her. They wanted her to form warm relationships with staff members as a starting point for her entry into the outside world. They also hoped to see how much Genie was capable of learning. Within months, she had learned about one hundred words, although she was still often difficult to understand.

The National Institute of Mental Health funded a research project to study Genie's **potential**. The researchers wanted to learn if "the clock could be turned back" for someone like her. They were especially anxious to see if a teenager who had never known language could still learn to talk. Even before Genie was discovered, scientists had been debating whether someone who couldn't speak by the time they reached puberty could ever become fluent in any language.

This girl is being given an IQ test similar to those Genie was given at various stages of her development.

While the research continued, Genie left the hospital twice to live with members of the health-care team and their families. She stayed with one of the psychologists for four years. Meanwhile, the question of whether Genie could be effectively helped as a patient and still remain a research subject loomed in the background.

Things did not always go smoothly for Genie in her new temporary homes. The young girl's emotions sometimes erupted in "silent storms of rage" during which she would tug and tear at her own body. But other days, Genie seemed to be making progress, and she even eventually started nursery school.

Yet all was not going well in other areas. While the psychologist she lived with tried to be both therapist and foster parent to Genie, the research he and the others had been expected to do began to take a back seat. In 1974, the National Institute of Mental Health stopped funding the Genie project, claiming that the research hadn't been done in a scientifically meaningful manner.

More Problems

The year after the research money stopped, the psychologist and his family announced that they could no longer act as Genie's foster family. This turn of events was just the start of a hailstorm of bad news for the girl. Language specialists noted that although she learned words, Genie was unable to form meaningful sentences or phrases. This lent support to the theory that language cannot be learned after a certain age.

In 1975, Genie went back to live with her mother. The woman had been cleared of child-abuse charges, and expressed a desire to finally care for her daughter. But the task proved too much for her, and Genie was sent to live in a foster home. Unfortunately, Genie experienced a series of unsuccessful foster-home placements in which she was abused, severely punished, and harassed.

At times, Genie was subjected to a level of cruelty that rivaled her early confinement. In one foster home, she was punished for vomiting. Genie was so upset that she responded as she had as a child—by remaining silent. One therapist claimed that Genie kept her mouth closed because she didn't want to vomit again and be punished. Genie was eventually put in an adult foster home in southern California. It was her sixth placement since the research project began.

Genie had a lot in common with "wild" youths of the past. All made some exciting progress, but stopped short of fulfilling their instructors' expectations or hopes. Each of these "wild" children had been exposed to unimaginable isolation early in their lives. Yet their rescue sometimes proved to be less than ideal as well. Despite the intense efforts of those around them, no "wild" children have ever fully fit into human society. They have always remained somewhere between civilization and a world that is uniquely their own.

GLOSSARY

ASSAILANT an attacker

CANINE of or relating to the family of animals that includes dogs

CIVILIZED exhibiting behavior that conforms to the rules and manners of a given society or culture

DEAF unable to hear

DELIRIOUS exhibiting behavior characterized by frenzy, hallucinations, and confusion

DEPOSE to remove someone from power and then take his or her place

EXCREMENT feces; waste matter released from the body

FERAL existing in a wild state; untamed

GUTTURAL a harsh sound coming from the throat

INFANTILE babylike

ISOLATION   the condition of being placed apart from others

LEGITIMATE   genuine

MENTALLY RETARDED   having below-normal mental ability that is present from birth and evidenced by slow development, learning difficulties, and problems in social adjustment

MISSIONARY   an individual sent by a church to convert, teach, or aid people in a foreign country

MUTE   unable to speak

OPTIMISTIC   hopeful; looking at things in a positive way

POTENTIAL   what is possible but not yet actual

PSYCHIATRIC   of or having to do with the treatment of mental illness

PSYCHOLOGIST   a person who studies the human mind to explain why people think, feel, and behave as they do

SOLITARY CONFINEMENT   imprisonment apart from others

SOW   a female pig

STY   a pen for pigs

UNKEMPT   untidy or disorderly

SOURCE NOTES

CHAPTER ONE

1. Paul Sieveking, "Forteana," *New Statesman & Society*, September 20, 1991, 35.

2. Ibid.

3. Ibid.

CHAPTER TWO

1. Douglas Keith Candland, *Feral Children & Clever Animals* (New York: Oxford University Press, 1993), 18.

2. Ibid., 21.

3. Ibid.

4. Jean-Marc Gaspard Itard, *The Wild Boy Of Aveyron* (Englewood Cliffs, New Jersey: Prentice Hall, 1962), 54.

5. Candland, 32.

6. "Secret of the Wild Child," *NOVA*, program #2112, October 18, 1994.

CHAPTER THREE

1. Candland, 46.

2. Ibid., 48.

3. Ibid., 49.

CHAPTER FOUR

1. The Reverend J. A. L. Singh and Robert M. Zingg, *Wolf-Children and Feral Man* (Hamden, Connecticut: Archon, 1966), 12.

2. Ibid., 28.

3. Candland, 60.

CHAPTER FIVE

1. "Secret of the Wild Child," *NOVA*, program #2112, October 18, 1994.

TO FIND OUT MORE

BOOKS

Brandenberg, Jim. **To the Top of the World;
Adventures with Arctic Wolves.** New York:
Walker & Company, 1993.

Burger, John R., and Lewis Gardner, eds. **Children of the Wild**.
New York: Messner, 1978.

Burroughs, Edgar Rice. **Tarzan of the Apes.** New York:
Ballantine Books, 1983.

Kipling, Rudyard. **The Jungle Book**. New York:
Viking Kestral, 1987.

Maclean, Charles. **The Wolf Children**. New York:
Hill and Wang, 1978.

Patent, Dorothy Hinshaw. **Dogs: The Wolf Within**.
Minneapolis: Carolrhoda Books, 1993.

Pringle, Laurence. **Feral: Tame Animals Gone Wild**.
New York: Macmillan, 1983.
Simon, Seymour. **Wolves**. New York: Harper Collins, 1993.

Yolen, Jane. **Children of the Wolf.** New York:
Viking Press, 1984.

FILM AND VIDEO

Greystoke, the Legend of Tarzan, Lord of the Apes.
Burbank, CA: available through Warner Home Video, 1984.
The fictional story of Tarzan, an infant boy who is raised by apes
but returns to society as an adult.

"Secret of the Wild Child," *NOVA* program #2112. October
18, 1994.
A documentary about children found living among animals
or in the wild.

The Wild Child (L'enfant sauvage).United Artists, 1970; available through Warner Home Video, 1991.
A fictional film based on the story of the "Wild Boy of Aveyron."

INDEX

Page numbers in *italics* indicate illustrations.

INDEX

ABOUT THE
AUTHOR

ELAINE LANDAU has a Bachelor of Arts degree in English and Journalism from New York University and a Masters degree in Library and Information Science from Pratt Institute. She has worked as a newspaper reporter, children's book editor, and a youth services librarian, but especially enjoys writing for young people.

Ms. Landau has written more than one hundred nonfiction books on various topics. She lives in Miami, Florida, with her husband, Norman, and son, Michael.